Frightful Flavors: The Boo-Tastic Halloween Cookbook:

Sink Your Teeth Into Ghoulish Goodies & Spooky Sweets

Lucian Stevens

Copyright © 2023 by Lucian Stevens

All rights reserved worldwide.

ISBN: 979-8862497137

No part of this book may be reproduced or transmitted in any form or by any means, electronic or mechanical, including photocopying, recording or by any information storage and retrieval system, without written permission from the publisher, except for the inclusion of brief quotations in a review.

Warning-Disclaimer

The purpose of this book is to educate and entertain. The author or publisher does not guarantee that anyone following the techniques, suggestions, ideas, or strategies will become successful. The author and publisher shall have neither liability nor responsibility to anyone for any loss or damage caused or alleged to be caused, directly or indirectly, by the information in this book.

CONTENTS

INTRODUCTION 5

GHASTLY APPETIZERS 8

Petrifying Pumpkin Soup 8

Mummy-Wrapped Hot Dogs 10

Haunted Jalapeño Poppers 12

Creepy Crawler Cheese Ball 14

Devilled Sticky Chicken Wings 16

EERIE ENTREES 18

Spine-Chilling Spaghetti with Eyeballs 18

Witch's Brew Stew 20

Monster Meatloaf 22

Zombie Brain Tacos 24

MACABRE SIDES 26

Witches' Fingers Breadsticks 26

Goblin Gooey Mac 'n' Cheese 28

Gravestone Garlic Mashed Potatoes 30

Ghostly Green Salad 32

SPOOKY SWEETS 34

Jack-o'-Lantern Cupcakes 34

Witch's Hat Cookies 36

Halloween Shortbread Bones...38

Vampire Blood Punch..40

Cursed Candy Apples 42

WICKED DRINKS...44

Pumpkin Spice Potion 44

Black Widow's Brew...46

Ghostly Elixir 48

Swamp Water Smoothie 50

TRICK-OR-TREAT GOODIES...52

Caramel Popcorn Balls 52

Homemade Candy Bars..54

Candy Corn Fudge 56

Spooky Snack Mix 58

POST-HALLOWEEN BREAKFAST 60

Candy Overload Pancakes 60

Witches' Brew Coffee...62

Ghostly Crepe Art 64

Pumpkin Spice French Toast..66

CONCLUSION 68

INTRODUCTION

Hello there, spooky friends!

Do you know what is the key to succeed at a party?

It's not about the tunes or the ambiance. While sprucing up the decor can certainly wow your guests, the real game-changer is the food!

Prepare to embark on a culinary journey that's both ghostly and delicious as I invite you to join us in celebrating the spookiest night of the year. Halloween, when the moon casts an eerie glow and the air is filled with the whispers of ghosts and the rustling of leaves, calls for a feast like no other. In this enchanted tome of recipes, I've gathered an array of hauntingly delightful dishes that will enchant your taste buds and captivate your imagination.

From ghastly appetizers that send shivers down your spine to spine-chilling main courses that will leave you spellbound, this cookbook is your ticket to becoming the ultimate Halloween host or hostess. You'll discover treats that are as delightful as frightful, ensuring that your Halloween gathering will be one for the books!

With step-by-step instructions, you'll easily recreate these spooktacular recipes, whether you're a seasoned chef or a kitchen novice. I've also sprinkled in some hauntingly fun facts and Halloween trivia to keep you entertained as you cook up a storm.

So grab your cauldron, don your witch's hat, and get ready to brew some magic in your kitchen. Whether you're hosting a kids gathering, planning a family fright night, or simply craving a taste of Halloween all year round, the Boo-tastic Halloween Cookbook is your go-to guide for creating memorable and mouthwatering moments.

Gather 'round, brave souls, and let the culinary enchantment begin. The spirits are stirring, and the cauldron is bubbling—Halloween has never tasted so good!

WHAT IS HALLOWEEN FOR ME?

Halloween is my favorite holiday. I love it because it's the one time of the year when I can let my imagination run wild. I love to think about all the different ways that food can be made to look like something else and then try to make those things happen in my kitchen.

The other great thing about Halloween is that it gives me an excuse to go all out with my costume and makeup. I usually spend weeks thinking about what I want to be for Halloween, and then I spend even more time putting together a costume that will blow everyone away.

My mom used to make me these amazing costumes every year, and she would help me make all sorts of things—like the best jack-o-lanterns ever! We'd spend hours outside carving pumpkins into scary faces that people could see from blocks away.

I hope you all have a great Halloween this year!

MY QUICK SUGGESTION OF HOW TO SPEND HALLOWEEN NIGHT AT HOME WITH YOUR FAMILY OR FRIENDS:

FIRST - Decorate your house with Halloween motifs: Decorate your house with terrifying faces made out of balloons: buy balloons, inflate them and paint the eyes and mouth or teeth with black marker. Make the scary but in a fun way.

SECOND - Prepare your table: buy an orange tablecloth and plates with edges appearing like spider webs. Also look for cutlery in the shape of bones.

THIRD - Place candles on the table with dim lighting and different Halloween objects in the shape of pumpkins, spiders, etc. Play spooky music to set the mode.

FORTH - Dress up as a bloody chef and encourage your guests to come in costumes.

FOOD: Prepare your scary menu:

Start with a platter with different appetizers of Mummy-Wrapped Hot Dogs, Haunted Jalapeño Poppers, Creepy Crawler Cheese Ball, and Devilled Sticky Chicken Wings arranged on a spooky-themed plate.

Serve a Ghostly Green Salad with eerie, glowing-green dressing.

Follow with Spine-Chilling Spaghetti with Eyeballs and Monster Meatloaf cut into slices and served with Gravestone Garlic Mashed Potatoes

Finish dinner with Jack-o'-Lantern Cupcakes decorated with cute pumpkin faces made of frosting.

DRINKS

Offer Pumpkin Spice Potion served in Halloween-themed mugs, accompanied by spooky-looking and refreshing Ghostly Elixir.

Enjoy a memorable Halloween dinner filled with deliciously eerie delights!

GHASTLY APPETIZERS

Petrifying Pumpkin Soup

The vibrant orange color and savory flavor of this Petrifying Pumpkin Soup will enchant your taste buds, while the floating "eyeballs" will send shivers down your spine. Perfect for setting the eerie tone of your Halloween feast.

Servings: 4

Prep + Cooking time: 30 minutes

Ingredients

2 cups canned pumpkin puree

1 cup vegetable broth

1/2 cup heavy cream

1 small onion, finely chopped

2 cloves garlic, minced

2 tablespoons butter

1/2 teaspoon ground nutmeg

Salt and pepper to taste

MOZZARELLA CHEESE BALLS (FOR THE "EYEBALLS")

BLACK OLIVES (FOR THE "PUPILS")

Fresh parsley (for garnish)

Directions

Step 1: Melt the butter in a large pot over medium heat. Add the chopped onion and minced garlic. Sauté until the onion becomes translucent, about 3-4 minutes.

Step 2: Stir in the canned pumpkin puree, vegetable broth, and ground nutmeg. Season with salt and pepper to taste. Bring the mixture to a simmer and let cook for 10-15 minutes, allowing the flavors to meld together.

Step 3: Reduce the heat to low heat and add the heavy cream. Next, simmer for an additional 5 minutes, stirring occasionally.

Step 4: Meanwhile the soup is simmering, prepare the "eyeballs." Take each mozzarella cheese ball and carefully slice a small hole into the center. Place a sliced black olive inside the hole to create the "pupil" of the eyeball.

Step 5: Serve the warm soup in individual bowls. Carefully float a mozzarella "eyeball" in the center of each bowl.

Step 6: Garnish with fresh parsley to add a touch of greenery to your spooky creation.

Step 7: Serve hot and watch your guests' eyes widen in amazement and fear!

TIPS

For an extra eerie effect, dim the lights and use LED candles as table decor while serving this Petrifying Pumpkin Soup.

Mummy-Wrapped Hot Dogs

These spooky Mummy-Wrapped Hot Dogs are the perfect Halloween party snack. They're easy to make and fun to eat, making them a hit with both kids and adults. Enjoy with your favorite dipping sauces for a ghoulishly good time!

Servings: 8 mummy-wrapped hot dogs

Prep + Cooking time: 20 minutes

Ingredients

Mustard or ketchup (for decorating mummy faces)

8 hot dogs

1 sheet of puff pastry, thawed

1 egg, beaten (for egg wash)

Directions

Step 1: Start by preheating your oven to 375°F. Line a baking sheet with parchment paper.

Step 2: Unroll the thawed puff pastry sheet and cut it into thin strips, about 1/4-inch wide.

Step 3: Wrap one hot dog with the puff pastry strips, leaving a small gap near the top to create the "mummy's face." Repeat this process with all the hot dogs.

Step 4: Brush the wrapped hot dogs with the beaten egg. This will give them a golden-brown finish when baked.

Step 5: Place the wrapped hot dogs on the prepared baking sheet and bake in the oven for 12-15 minutes or until the puff pastry is golden and puffed up.

Step 6: Once out of the oven, let the mummy-wrapped hot dogs cool slightly before adding the "mummy faces."

Step 7: Using mustard or ketchup, dot two small eyes on each mummy's face to create a spooky look.

Step 8: Serve your Mummy-Wrapped Hot Dogs with your favorite dipping sauces, and watch them disappear at your Halloween party!

TIPS

Feel free to get creative with the mummy faces! You can make them as spooky or silly as you like using condiments.

Haunted Jalapeño Poppers

Prepare to spice up your Halloween night with these fiery, ghostly Haunted Jalapeño Poppers. These devilishly delicious snacks bring the heat and the haunting, making them the perfect treat for brave souls. Watch out for the surprise lurking inside each popper!

Servings: 16 jalapeño poppers

Prep + Cooking time: 30 minutes

Ingredients

1/2 cup cooked and crumbled bacon (for the fiery "souls")

Red food coloring (for the "haunting" effect)

8 fresh jalapeño peppers

8 oz cream cheese, softened

1 cup shredded cheddar cheese

1/2 teaspoon garlic powder

Salt and pepper to taste

1 cup breadcrumbs

2 eggs, beaten

Cooking oil for frying

Blue cheese dressing

Directions

Step 1: Slice each jalapeño pepper in half lengthwise, and carefully remove the seeds and membranes. These fiery spirits are about to get a chilling makeover!

Step 2: In a mixing bowl, combine the softened cream cheese, shredded cheddar cheese, crumbled bacon (our fiery "souls"), garlic powder, salt, and pepper. Mix until well combined.

Step 3: Fill each jalapeño half with the cream cheese mixture, creating a deliciously haunting surprise for your taste buds.

Step 4: In a separate bowl, mix a few drops of red food coloring into the beaten eggs to create a blood-red egg wash.

Step 5: Dip each filled jalapeño into the red egg wash, coating them completely.

Step 6: Roll the coated jalapeños in breadcrumbs, ensuring they are well-covered. This will give them a crispy, eerie exterior.

Step 7: Heat cooking oil in a deep skillet to 350°F. It's time to exorcise these jalapeño spirits by frying them until golden brown. This should take about 3-4 minutes.

Step 8: Carefully remove your haunted jalapeño poppers from the oil and let them drain on paper towels to rid them of any excess fat.

Step 9: Serve your Haunted Jalapeño Poppers with blue cheese dressing to help brave souls cool off after a fiery encounter with these spicy phantoms.

TIPS

To add an extra element of surprise, consider leaving one or two jalapeño poppers uncolored for your guests to discover the "ghost pepper" among them!

Creepy Crawler Cheese Ball

Prepare to be spellbound by the sinister charm of our Creepy Crawler Cheese Ball. This spine-tingling appetizer is delicious and adds a ghoulish touch to your Halloween spread. Hidden beneath its cheesy exterior are many eerie surprises that delight your guests.

Servings: 8-10

Prep + Cooking time: 20 minutes + Chiling time

Ingredients

8 oz cream cheese, softened

1 cup shredded cheddar cheese

1/2 cup grated Parmesan cheese

1/4 cup finely chopped black olives

1/4 cup finely chopped green onions

1/4 cup finely chopped red bell pepper

1 teaspoon garlic powder

1/2 teaspoon onion powder

Salt and pepper to taste

BLACK OLIVES (FOR THE "CREEPY CRAWLERS")

PRETZEL STICKS (FOR THE "SPIDER LEGS")

Directions

Step 1: In a large mixing bowl, combine the softened cream cheese, shredded cheddar cheese, grated Parmesan cheese, chopped black olives, chopped green onions, chopped red bell pepper, garlic powder, onion powder, salt, and pepper. Mix until all ingredients are well incorporated. This will be the body of your cheese ball.

Step 2: Shape the cheese mixture into a ball resembling the body of a mysterious creature lurking in the shadows.

Step 3: Place the cheese ball on a serving platter.

Step 4: To create the "creepy crawlers," take whole black olives and slice them in half lengthwise. Press each half olive gently into the cheese ball, positioning them as if they're emerging from the depths of darkness.

Step 5: For an extra eerie effect, insert pretzel sticks into the sides of the cheese ball to form "spider legs" that give your creepy crawlers a spooky appearance.

Step 6: Chill the Creepy Crawler Cheese Ball in the refrigerator for at least 50-60 minutes to allow the flavors to meld together and the cheese ball to firm up.

Step 7: Before serving, surround the cheese ball with your favorite crackers or bread slices, inviting your guests to unravel the mysteries hidden within. Enjoy the delicious fright!

TIPS

You can customize your Creepy Crawler Cheese Ball by using different types of olives for the "crawlers" or adding hot sauce to give it an extra kick of flavor.

Devilled Sticky Chicken Wings

These fiery delights are not for the faint of heart. They pack a punch with spicy seasonings that will leave you craving more. Perfect for heat-seekers who dare to take on the devil.

Servings: 4

Prep + Cooking time: 45 minutes

Ingredients

2 lb chicken wings

2 tablespoons sriracha sauce

2 tablespoons honey

1 teaspoon cayenne pepper

1 teaspoon paprika

1/2 teaspoon garlic powder

1/2 teaspoon onion powder

Salt and black pepper to taste

Chopped fresh cilantro (for garnish)

Lime wedges (for a zesty kick)

Directions

Step 1: Start by preheating your oven to 425°F. Line a baking sheet with aluminum foil. Place a wire rack on top of the lined baking sheet.

Step 2: In a large bowl, combine the sriracha sauce, honey, cayenne pepper, paprika, garlic powder, onion powder, salt, and black pepper. Stir until the mixture forms a tantalizing glaze.

Step 3: Add the chicken wings to the bowl with the spicy glaze and toss them until they are generously coated.

Step 4: Arrange the coated wings on the wire rack on the baking sheet, ensuring they are spaced out evenly for crispy perfection.

Step 5: Bake the wings in the preheated oven for 25-30 minutes, turning them once midway through, until they achieve a mouthwatering golden crispiness.

Step 6: As the wings are hot and ready to sizzle, garnish them with chopped fresh cilantro and serve them with lime wedges for an extra zesty kick.

TIPS

These wings are spellbindingly versatile. Add more sriracha for an extra fiery enchantment or a drizzle of honey for a sweeter spell.

EERIE ENTREES

Spine-Chilling Spaghetti with Eyeballs

Get ready to cast a spell of flavor with these spaghetti and let them work their magic on your taste buds!

Servings: 4

Prep + Cooking time: 45 minutes

Ingredients

FOR THE MEATBALLS:

1 lb ground beef

1/2 cup breadcrumbs

1/4 cup grated Parmesan cheese

1/4 cup milk

1/4 cup finely chopped onion

1 egg

1 teaspoon garlic powder

1 teaspoon dried oregano

Salt and black pepper to taste

FOR THE EYEBALL "IRISES":

Pitted black olives, sliced into rounds

FOR THE SPAGHETTI:

8 oz spaghetti

1 tablespoon olive oil

2 cups marinara sauce

Fresh basil leaves (for garnish)

Grated Parmesan cheese (for serving)

Directions

Step 1: Start by preheating your oven to 375°F. Grease a baking sheet.

Step 2: In a large bowl, combine ground beef, breadcrumbs, grated Parmesan cheese, milk, chopped onion, egg, garlic powder, dried oregano, salt, and black pepper. Mix until well combined.

Step 3: Shape the mixture into meatballs of your desired size, each about the size of an eyeball.

Step 4: Place the meatballs on the greased baking sheet and bake them in the preheated oven for 15-20 minutes or until they are cooked through.

Step 5: While the meatballs are baking, cook the spaghetti according to the package instructions until al dente. Drain and toss with olive oil to prevent sticking.

Step 6: Warm the marinara sauce in a large pan over low heat.

Step 7: To create the "eyeballs," gently press a slice of pitted black olive into the center of each meatball.

Step 8: To serve, place a portion of cooked spaghetti on each plate, top it with marinara sauce, and arrange the meatball "eyeballs" on top. Garnish with fresh basil leaves and a sprinkle of grated Parmesan cheese for added flavor.

TIPS

These wings are spellbindingly versatile. Adjust the heat to your liking by adding more sriracha for an extra fiery enchantment or a drizzle of honey for a sweeter spell.

Witch's Brew Stew

Dive into the enchanting depths of our Witch's Brew Stew, a spellbinding concoction perfect for a bewitching Halloween feast. This hearty stew combines various ingredients that will cast a delicious spell on your taste buds. Served in a cauldron and topped with eerie "eyeballs," it's an extremely fun dish that captures the season's spirit.

Servings: 4

Prep + Cooking time: 1 hour 50 minutes

Ingredients

FOR THE STEW:

1 lb boneless beef stew meat, cubed

1 tablespoon olive oil

1 onion, finely chopped

2 cloves garlic, minced

2 carrots, peeled and sliced

2 potatoes, peeled and diced

1 cup butternut squash, peeled and diced

1 cup green beans, trimmed and cut into bite-sized pieces

4 cups beef broth

1 cup tomato sauce

1 teaspoon dried thyme

1 teaspoon dried rosemary

Salt and black pepper to taste

FOR THE "EYEBALLS":

Hard-boiled eggs, peeled and halved

Pimiento-stuffed green olives

Red food coloring

Directions

Step 1: In a large pot, heat the olive oil over medium-high heat. Add the cubed beef stew meat and brown it on all sides. Remove the meat from the pot and set it aside.

Step 2: In the same pot, add the chopped onion and minced garlic. Sauté until the onion becomes translucent.

Step 3: Return the browned beef to the pot, and add the carrots, potatoes, butternut squash, and green beans.

Step 4: Pour in the beef broth and tomato sauce. Add the dried thyme and dried rosemary. Season with salt and black pepper to taste.

Step 5: Bring the mixture to a boil, then reduce the heat to low. Cover and simmer for approximately 1 hour, or until the meat is tender and the vegetables are cooked through.

Step 6: While the stew is simmering, prepare the "eyeballs." Take the hard-boiled eggs and cut them in half lengthwise. Place a pimiento-stuffed green olive in the center of each half to create the "iris" of the eyeball. Use a small amount of red food coloring to add spooky "veins" to the egg whites.

Step 7: Once the stew is ready, ladle it into serving bowls or a cauldron, and top each serving with a creepy "eyeball."

TIPS

Customize your Witch's Brew Stew with additional seasonal vegetables or your favorite herbs and spices to create your own magical potion.

Monster Meatloaf

Prepare to unleash the culinary creature within with our Monster Meatloaf! This monstrous creation is a fusion of ground meats, savory seasonings, and a ghoulish glaze that's as delicious as it is frightful. Crafted in the shape of a legendary Halloween monster, it's a show-stopping centerpiece for your spooky feast.

Servings: 6 | Prep + Cooking time: 1 hour 35 minutes

Ingredients

FOR THE MEATLOAF:

1 lb ground beef

1/2 lb ground pork

1/2 lb ground veal

1 onion, finely chopped

2 cloves garlic, minced

1 cup breadcrumbs

1/2 cup milk

1/4 cup ketchup

1/4 cup grated Parmesan cheese

2 eggs

1 teaspoon dried oregano

1 teaspoon dried basil

Salt and black pepper to taste

FOR THE GLAZE:

1/2 cup ketchup

2 tablespoons brown sugar

1 tablespoon Dijon mustard

FOR DECORATION:

Sliced bell peppers, olives, or vegetables of your choice for creating "monster" features

Directions

Step 1: Start by preheating your oven to 350°F. Line a baking sheet with parchment paper.

Step 2: In a large mixing bowl, combine the ground beef, ground pork, ground veal, chopped onion, minced garlic, breadcrumbs, milk, ketchup, grated Parmesan cheese, eggs, dried oregano, dried basil, salt, and black pepper. Mix until all the ingredients are thoroughly combined.

Step 3: Shape the meat mixture into a monstrous creature of your choice on the prepared baking sheet. You can create a traditional meatloaf shape or get creative by crafting a unique monster shape.

Step 4: In a small bowl, mix the ingredients for the glaze: ketchup, brown sugar, and Dijon mustard. Brush the glaze generously over the entire surface of your meatloaf monster.

Step 5: Use sliced bell peppers, olives, or other vegetables to decorate your meatloaf monster, creating "eyes," "noses," "mouths," or any other eerie features you like.

Step 6: Bake the Monster Meatloaf in the preheated oven for approximately 1 hour and 15 minutes, or until it's cooked through and has a rich, caramelized glaze.

Step 7: Once done, carefully transfer your edible monster masterpiece to a serving platter and let it rest for a few minutes before slicing.

TIPS

Serve your Monster Meatloaf with mashed potatoes and green beans for a complete and hauntingly delicious Halloween dinner.

Zombie Brain Tacos

Prepare to terrify and tantalize your taste buds with these creepy yet satisfying Zombie Brain Tacos!

Servings: 4

Prep + Cooking time: 50 minutes

Ingredients

FOR THE "ZOMBIE BRAIN" FILLING:

1 lb ground beef

1 onion, finely chopped

2 cloves garlic, minced

1 can (14 oz) refried beans

1 packet taco seasoning mix

1/2 cup water

Salt and black pepper to taste

FOR THE "BRAIN MATTER" TOPPING:

1/2 cup sour cream

1/4 cup mayonnaise

Green food coloring

Red food coloring

Blue food coloring

FOR ASSEMBLING THE TACOS:

8 taco shells

Shredded lettuce

Diced tomatoes

Sliced black olives

Shredded cheddar cheese

Red food coloring

Directions

Step 1: In a large skillet over medium heat, cook the ground beef, chopped onion, and minced garlic until the beef is browned and the onion is translucent. Drain any excess grease.

Step 2: Stir in the refried beans, taco seasoning mix, water, salt, and black pepper. Cook and stir until the mixture is heated through and well combined. Set it aside.

Step 3: In a separate bowl, prepare the "Brain Matter" topping by combining sour cream and mayonnaise. To create the eerie green hue, add a few drops of green food coloring. For added authenticity, add a drop of red and blue food coloring to mimic brain-like streaks. Mix until the color is swirled and resembles zombie brain matter.

Step 4: Warm the taco shells in the oven according to the package instructions.

Step 5: To assemble your Zombie Brain Tacos, spoon the ground beef and bean mixture into each taco shell. Top with shredded lettuce, diced tomatoes, sliced black olives, and a generous dollop of the "Brain Matter" topping.

Step 6: Serve your Zombie Brain Tacos to your unsuspecting guests and watch as they savor the taste of deliciously sinister brain-inspired tacos.

TIPS

Customize your Zombie Brain Tacos with additional toppings like guacamole, jalapeños, or hot sauce to add an extra kick to your zombie feast.

MACABRE SIDES

Witches' Fingers Breadsticks

Get ready to enchant your Halloween guests with these eerie and delicious Witches' Fingers Breadsticks, perfect for dipping and dining on the spookiest night of the year!

Servings: 12 breadsticks

Prep + Cooking time: 50 minutes

Ingredients

FOR THE BREADSTICKS:

1 pound pizza dough (store-bought or homemade)

12 whole blanched almonds (for "nails")

1 egg, beaten (for egg wash)

Black sesame seeds (for added texture)

FOR THE "BLOOD" DIPPING SAUCE:

1/2 cup marinara sauce

Directions

Step 1: Start by preheating your oven to 375°F. Line a baking sheet with parchment paper.

Step 2: Divide the pizza dough into 12 equal portions and roll each portion into a thin rope, about 6-7 inches in length.

Step 3: Gently press one blanched almond into the tip of each dough rope to create the "nail" of the witch's finger.

Step 4: Use a knife to make several shallow, irregular slashes along the length of each dough rope to give the appearance of wrinkled and knotted fingers.

Step 5: Arrange the prepared dough ropes on the parchment-lined baking sheet, spacing them out evenly.

Step 6: Brush the dough ropes with the beaten egg to create a golden, slightly glossy finish.

Step 7: Sprinkle black sesame seeds over the breadsticks to add texture and an eerie touch.

Step 8: Bake in the oven for 15-18 minutes, or until the breadsticks are golden brown and fully baked.

Step 9: While the breadsticks are baking, heat the marinara sauce in a small saucepan over low heat, creating the "blood" dipping sauce.

Step 10: Once baked, remove the breadsticks from the oven and let them cool slightly.

Step 11: Serve your Witches' Fingers Breadsticks with the warm marinara "blood" sauce on the side for a ghoulishly delightful dipping experience.

TIPS

You can customize your breadsticks by adding dried herbs like rosemary or thyme to the dough for extra flavor.

Goblin Gooey Mac 'n' Cheese

Venture into the mysterious realm of goblins with our Goblin Gooey Mac 'n' Cheese. This spine-tingling twist on a classic comfort dish combines cooked macaroni with a gooey, cheesy sauce that's infused with a hint of enchantment. Your taste buds will be spellbound by this irresistible Halloween treat.

Servings: 6

Prep + Cooking time: 45 minutes

Ingredients

FOR THE MAC 'N' CHEESE:

12 oz elbow macaroni

1/4 cup unsalted butter

1/4 cup all-purpose flour

2 cups whole milk

2 cups shredded cheddar cheese

1/2 cup shredded mozzarella cheese

1/2 cup grated Parmesan cheese

1/2 teaspoon garlic powder

1/2 teaspoon onion powder

Salt and black pepper to taste

FOR THE GOBLIN GARNISH:

Green food coloring

Edible googly eyes

Sliced black olives

Directions

Step 1: Cook the elbow macaroni according to the package instructions until al dente. Drain and set aside.

Step 2: In a large saucepan over medium heat, melt the unsalted butter.

Step 3: Stir in the all-purpose flour to create a roux and cook for a minute or two until it's golden and fragrant.

Step 4: Slowly whisk in the whole milk, ensuring there are no lumps in the sauce. Cook and stir continuously until the mixture thickens and begins to bubble.

Step 5: Reduce the heat to low, then stir in the shredded cheddar cheese, shredded mozzarella cheese, and grated Parmesan cheese. Continue to stir until the cheese is fully melted and the sauce is smooth.

Step 6: Season the cheese sauce with garlic powder, onion powder, salt, and black pepper. Adjust the seasonings to taste.

Step 7: Add a few drops of green food coloring to the cheese sauce to give it a goblin-esque hue. Mix well until the color is evenly distributed.

Step 8: Combine the cooked macaroni with the green, gooey cheese sauce and stir until the macaroni is thoroughly coated.

Step 9: To serve, dish out your Goblin Gooey Mac 'n' Cheese into individual bowls or a large serving dish.

Step 10: Add a playful goblin garnish by topping each serving with edible googly eyes and sliced black olives for a whimsical and spooky touch.

TIPS

For an extra kick of flavor, consider adding diced jalapeños or cooked bacon bits to your Goblin Gooey Mac 'n' Cheese.

Gravestone Garlic Mashed Potatoes

Prepare to descend into the eerie depths of flavor with our Gravestone Garlic Mashed Potatoes. These hauntingly delicious mashed potatoes are infused with the robust essence of roasted garlic, transforming an ordinary side dish into a spine-chilling masterpiece to leave your taste buds bewitched.

Servings: 6

Prep + Cooking time: 40 minutes

Ingredients

FOR THE GARLIC MASHED POTATOES:

2 lbs russet potatoes, peeled and cubed

4 cloves garlic, peeled

1/2 cup unsalted butter

1/2 cup milk

Salt and black pepper to taste

Chopped fresh chives (for garnish)

FOR THE GRAVEYARD PRESENTATION:

Store-bought edible gravestone decorations or create your own with crackers or bread

Directions

Step 1: Place the peeled and cubed potatoes in a large pot and cover them with cold water. Add a pinch of salt and bring the water to a boil over high heat.

Step 2: Once the water is boiling, reduce the heat to medium-high and simmer the potatoes for about 15-20 minutes or until they are tender and easily pierced with a fork.

Step 3: While the potatoes are cooking, preheat your oven to 375°F.

Step 4: In a small oven-safe dish, place the peeled garlic cloves and drizzle them with a bit of olive oil. Roast them in the preheated oven for about 15 minutes or until they are soft and slightly golden.

Step 5: Drain the cooked potatoes thoroughly and return them to the pot.

Step 6: Mash the potatoes using a potato masher or a ricer.

Step 7: Squeeze the roasted garlic cloves into the mashed potatoes and add the unsalted butter. Continue to mash and mix until the butter is fully melted and the potatoes are creamy.

Step 8: Pour in the milk, a little at a time, and continue to mash and mix until the mashed potatoes reach your desired creamy consistency.

Step 9: Season the Gravestone Garlic Mashed Potatoes with salt and black pepper to taste.

Step 10: Serve your mashed potatoes in a spooky graveyard presentation by arranging edible gravestone decorations or creating your own tombstones with crackers or bread.

Step 11: Garnish the mashed potatoes with chopped fresh chives to add a pop of color and freshness.

TIPS

For a richer flavor, you can also add shredded cheese, such as cheddar or Parmesan, to your mashed potatoes.

Ghostly Green Salad

Evoke the spirit of Halloween with our Ghostly Green Salad, a refreshing and eerie dish that's perfect for your Halloween celebration. This vibrant green salad is adorned with ghostly mozzarella cheese shapes, creating a spooktacular visual delight that's as fun to make as it is to eat.

Servings: 4

Prep + Cooking time: 15 minutes

Ingredients

FOR THE SALAD:

6 cups mixed greens (such as spinach, arugula, and lettuce)

1 cup cucumber, thinly sliced

1 cup green grapes, halved

1/2 cup green bell pepper, diced

1/4 cup red onion, thinly sliced

FOR THE GHOSTLY MOZZARELLA SHAPES:

Fresh mozzarella cheese slices or balls

Small black olives, pitted

FOR THE GREEN GODDESS DRESSING:

1/2 cup mayonnaise

1/2 cup sour cream

1/4 cup fresh parsley leaves, chopped

1/4 cup fresh chives, chopped

2 tablespoons fresh tarragon leaves, chopped

2 tablespoons fresh lemon juice

1 garlic clove, minced

Salt and black pepper to taste

Directions

Step 1: In a large salad bowl, combine the mixed greens, sliced cucumber, halved green grapes, diced green bell pepper, and thinly sliced red onion. Toss to mix the ingredients evenly.

Step 2: To create the Ghostly Mozzarella Shapes, use a ghost-shaped cookie cutter to cut out ghost figures from the mozzarella slices or balls. For the eyes, use small pitted black olives and slice them into rounds.

Step 3: Gently place the mozzarella ghost figures on top of the salad, scattering them evenly for a spooky presentation.

Step 4: In a separate bowl, prepare the Green Goddess Dressing. Combine mayonnaise, sour cream, chopped fresh parsley, chopped fresh chives, chopped fresh tarragon, fresh lemon juice, minced garlic, salt, and black pepper. Mix until the dressing is smooth and well combined.

Step 5: Drizzle the Green Goddess Dressing over the salad or serve it on the side for your guests to add as desired.

Step 6: Serve your Ghostly Green Salad as a creepy and refreshing addition to your Halloween spread.

TIPS

You can customize your Ghostly Green Salad by adding other green-hued ingredients like avocado slices, green apples, or edamame for extra flavor and texture.

SPOOKY SWEETS

Jack-o'-Lantern Cupcakes

Light up your Halloween party with these delightful Jack-o'-Lantern Cupcakes that are as fun to decorate as they are to eat!

Servings: 12 cupcakes | Prep + Cooking time: 60 minutes

Ingredients

FOR THE CUPCAKES:

1 1/2 cups all-purpose flour

1 1/2 teaspoons baking powder

1/4 teaspoon salt

1/2 cup unsalted butter, softened

1 cup granulated sugar

2 large eggs

1 teaspoon vanilla extract

1/2 cup whole milk

FOR THE FROSTING:

1/2 cup unsalted butter, softened

2 cups powdered sugar

2 tablespoons milk

Orange food coloring

FOR DECORATING:

Green and black decorating gel

Small candy eyes

Orange sprinkles

Directions

Step 1: Start by preheating your oven to 350°F. Line a cupcake tin with paper liners.

Step 2: In a bowl, whisk together the all-purpose flour, baking powder, and salt. Set aside. In a separate bowl, cream together the softened unsalted butter and granulated sugar until light and fluffy.

Step 3: Add the eggs one at a time, mixing well after each addition. Stir in the vanilla extract. Gradually add the dry ingredients to the wet ingredients, alternating with the whole milk, beginning and ending with the dry ingredients. Mix until just combined; be careful not to overmix.

Step 4: Divide the cupcake batter evenly among the paper liners, filling each about two-thirds full. Bake in the oven for 18-20 minutes or until a toothpick inserted into the center of a cupcake comes out clean. Allow the cupcakes to cool completely on a wire rack.

Step 5: In the meantime, prepare the frosting by creaming together the softened unsalted butter, powdered sugar, and milk until smooth and fluffy. Add orange food coloring to achieve the desired pumpkin hue.

Step 6: Once the cupcakes are cooled, spread or pipe the orange frosting on top of each cupcake.

Step 7: To decorate, use green decorating gel to create pumpkin stems on the top of each cupcake. Use black decorating gel to draw jack-o'-lantern faces on the cupcakes. You can get creative with different expressions!

Step 8: Add small candy eyes or orange sprinkles to the cupcakes to enhance their charm. Let the decorated cupcakes set before serving.

TIPS

Feel free to customize your jack-o'-lantern faces with various expressions, from spooky to silly, to create a unique set of cupcakes.

Witch's Hat Cookies

Conjure up some Halloween magic with these delightful Witch's Hat Cookies that are sure to enchant your taste buds and captivate your guests!

Servings: 24 cookies | Prep + Cooking time: 50 minutes

Ingredients

FOR THE COOKIES:

1 1/2 cups all-purpose flour

1/2 cup unsweetened cocoa powder

1/2 teaspoon baking powder

1/4 teaspoon salt

1/2 cup unsalted butter, softened

1 cup granulated sugar

1 large egg

1 teaspoon vanilla extract

2 tablespoons whole milk

FOR DECORATING:

24 chocolate kisses, unwrapped

Orange and black decorating gel

Directions

Step 1: Start by preheating your oven to 350°F. Line a baking sheet with parchment paper.

Step 2: In a bowl, whisk together the all-purpose flour, cocoa powder, baking powder, and salt. Set aside. In another bowl, cream together the softened unsalted butter and granulated sugar until light and fluffy.

Step 3: Add the egg and vanilla extract to the butter mixture and mix until well combined.

Step 4: Gradually add the dry ingredients to the wet ingredients, alternating with the whole milk, beginning and ending with the dry ingredients. Mix until a soft dough forms.

Step 5: Roll the cookie dough into 24 small balls, each about 1 inch in diameter.

Step 6: Place the cookie dough balls onto the prepared baking sheet, spacing them about 2 inches apart.

Step 7: Flatten each dough ball slightly with the bottom of a glass to form a cookie shape.

Step 8: Bake in the oven for 10-12 minutes or until the cookies are set.

Step 9: Remove the cookies from the oven and immediately press a chocolate kiss into the center of each cookie, creating the "witch's hat."

Step 10: Allow the cookies to cool on the baking sheet for a few minutes before transferring them to a wire rack to cool completely.

Step 11: Once the cookies are completely cooled, use orange decorating gel to create a band around the base of each "witch's hat" and a buckle in the center.

Step 12: Use black decorating gel to draw a belt around the band and any additional decorative details you like.

Step 13: Add small colorful candies or sprinkles to the cookies for extra flair.

TIPS

Get creative with different colors and patterns for your witch's hat cookies to create a charming array of edible witchy accessories.

Halloween Shortbread Bones

Serve these Halloween Shortbread Bones at your gathering, and watch as your guests nibble away on these delectable skeletal treats. They're a delightfully frightful addition to any Halloween table!

Servings: 24 cookies

Prep + Cooking time: 50 minutes

Ingredients

FOR THE SHORTBREAD BONES:

1 cup (2 sticks) unsalted butter, softened

1/2 cup granulated sugar

2 cups all-purpose flour

1/4 teaspoon salt

1 teaspoon vanilla extract

1/2 teaspoon almond extract

Powdered sugar (for dusting)

FOR DECORATING:

White royal icing or white chocolate for "gluing" the bones together

Red gel icing for a "bloody" effect

Directions

Step 1: In a mixing bowl, cream together the softened unsalted butter and granulated sugar until light and fluffy.

Step 2: Add the vanilla extract and almond extract to the butter mixture and mix until well combined.

Step 3: In a separate bowl, whisk together the all-purpose flour and salt.

Step 4: Gradually add the dry ingredients to the butter mixture, mixing until a soft dough forms.

Step 5: Divide the dough into two portions and shape each portion into a disc. Wrap them in plastic wrap and refrigerate for at least 1 hour or until the dough is firm.

Step 6: Start by preheating your oven to 325°F. Line a baking sheet with parchment paper.

Step 7: On a lightly floured surface, roll out one portion of the dough to a 1/4-inch thickness. Use bone-shaped cookie cutters to cut out bone shapes from the dough. Transfer the bone shapes to the prepared baking sheet, leaving a small space between each.

Step 8: Bake in the oven for 15-18 minutes or until the edges of the cookies are lightly golden. Remove from the oven and let them cool on the baking sheet for a few minutes before transferring them to a wire rack to cool completely.

Step 9: Once the cookies are cool, you can use white royal icing or melted white chocolate to "glue" the bone pieces together, creating realistic-looking bone structures. Add a touch of red gel icing for a spooky "bloody" effect.

Step 10: Dust the Halloween Shortbread Bones with powdered sugar to give them an eerie, bone-like appearance.

TIPS

Get creative with your decorating by adding cracks, details, or even "dirt" with edible food colors to make your shortbread bones look even spookier.

Vampire Blood Punch

Embrace the darkness with Vampire Blood Punch, a Halloween drink that will leave your guests thirsting for more!

Servings: 10

Prep + Cooking time: 10 minutes

Ingredients

FOR THE VAMPIRE BLOOD PUNCH:

4 cups cranberry juice

2 cups pomegranate juice

1 cup orange juice

1/2 cup pineapple juice

1/4 cup grenadine syrup

1/4 cup fresh lime juice

4 cups sparkling water or club soda, chilled

Fresh blackberries (for garnish)

Ice cubes

FOR THE VAMPIRE FANG GARNISH:

Plastic vampire fangs (available at party supply stores)

Directions

Step 1: In a large punch bowl or pitcher, combine the cranberry juice, pomegranate juice, orange juice, pineapple juice, grenadine syrup, and fresh lime juice. Stir until well mixed.

Step 2: Just before serving, gently pour in the chilled sparkling water or club soda to add a fizzy element to the punch.

Step 3: Add ice cubes to the punch to keep it cool without diluting the flavors.

Step 4: To create a spooky vampire garnish, attach plastic vampire fangs to the rim of each glass. These can be found at party supply stores and add a playful touch to your Vampire Blood Punch.

Step 5: Pour the punch into glasses, garnishing each with a few fresh blackberries for an eerie, blood-red effect.

Step 6: Serve your Vampire Blood Punch to your guests, and watch as they indulge in this hauntingly delicious elixir.

TIPS

For an adult version of this punch, consider adding a splash of vodka or rum to individual servings.

Cursed Candy Apples

Beware the spellbinding allure of Cursed Candy Apples as you savor their wickedly sweet magic on Halloween night!

Servings: 4

Prep + Cooking time: 15 minutes

Ingredients

FOR THE CANDY APPLES:

6 medium-sized apples

2 cups granulated sugar

1/2 cup light corn syrup

1/2 cup water

Red food coloring

Candy apple sticks or wooden skewers

FOR DECORATING:

Edible glitter or edible gold dust

Black decorating gel

Halloween-themed sprinkles

Directions

Step 1: Wash and dry the apples thoroughly. Remove any stems and insert candy apple sticks or wooden skewers into the top center of each apple. Set aside.

Step 2: In a heavy-bottomed saucepan, combine granulated sugar, light corn syrup, and water over medium-high heat. Stir until the sugar is dissolved.

Step 3: Bring the mixture to a boil, then reduce the heat to medium-low. Insert a candy thermometer into the mixture and continue to cook without stirring until it reaches the hard crack stage, which is around 300°F. This may take about 10-15 minutes.

Step 4: Once the mixture reaches the desired temperature, remove it from the heat and stir in a few drops of red food coloring until you achieve the desired deep red hue.

Step 5: Working quickly but carefully, dip each apple into the hot candy mixture, coating it evenly. Allow any excess candy to drip back into the saucepan.

Step 6: Place the candy-coated apples on a parchment paper-lined baking sheet to cool and harden.

Step 7: Decorate the candy apples while the coating is still slightly tacky. Sprinkle them with edible glitter, edible gold dust, or Halloween-themed sprinkles. Create eerie faces or designs using black decorating gel.

Step 8: Let the Cursed Candy Apples cool completely and harden before serving. This may take about 30 minutes.

TIPS

To add a sinister twist, you can also drizzle melted dark chocolate over the candy-coated apples.

WICKED DRINKS

Pumpkin Spice Potion

Delight in the magical flavors of fall with this Pumpkin Spice Potion, a brew that captures the essence of autumn in every sip!

Servings: 4

Prep + Cooking time: 20 minutes

Ingredients

FOR THE PUMPKIN SPICE POTION:

2 cups whole milk

1 cup canned pumpkin puree

1/4 cup granulated sugar

2 teaspoons pumpkin pie spice

1 teaspoon vanilla extract

1/2 cup brewed strong coffee or espresso

FOR GARNISH:

Whipped cream

Ground cinnamon or pumpkin pie spice

Cinnamon sticks or star anise

Directions

Step 1: In a medium saucepan over medium heat, combine the whole milk, canned pumpkin puree, granulated sugar, pumpkin pie spice, and vanilla extract. Whisk the mixture until it's well combined.

Step 2: Heat the mixture, stirring occasionally, until it's hot but not boiling. This should take about 5-7 minutes.

Step 3: Add a coffee kick to your potion, brew a strong cup of coffee or espresso and stir it into the pumpkin mixture.

Step 4: Once the Pumpkin Spice Potion is hot and well mixed, remove it from the heat.

Step 5: Carefully pour the potion into mugs or glasses, leaving some space at the top for garnishes.

Step 6: Top each serving with a dollop of whipped cream and a sprinkle of ground cinnamon or pumpkin pie spice.

Step 7: Add a cinnamon stick or a star anise to each mug for an extra touch of autumnal flair.

Step 8: Serve your Pumpkin Spice Potion to your guests and let them savor the warm, cozy flavors of the season.

TIPS

Customize your potion by adjusting the sweetness to your liking. You can also substitute whole milk with almond milk or oat milk for a dairy-free version.

Black Widow's Brew

Embrace the allure of the night with Black Widow's Brew, a dark and captivating potion that will enchant your Halloween gathering.

Servings: 6

Preparation time: 10 minutes

Ingredients

FOR THE BLACK WIDOW'S BREW:

2 cups blackberries

1 cup blackcurrant juice

1/2 cup dark rum

1/4 cup simple syrup

1 tablespoon fresh lemon juice

Crushed ice

Fresh blackberries and lemon slices for garnish

FOR SIMPLE SYRUP:

1 cup granulated sugar

1 cup water

Directions

Step 1: Prepare the simple syrup by combining equal parts granulated sugar and water in a saucepan. Heat over medium heat, stirring until the sugar is completely dissolved. Allow the syrup to cool before using it in the brew.

Step 2: In a blender, combine the blackberries, blackcurrant juice, dark rum, simple syrup, and fresh lemon juice.

Step 3: Blend the mixture until it's smooth and well combined.

Step 4: Fill glasses with crushed ice to your liking.

Step 5: Pour the Black Widow's Brew over the crushed ice in each glass.

Step 6: Garnish each glass with a few fresh blackberries and a slice of lemon for a touch of elegance and mystique.

Step 7: Serve your Black Widow's Brew to your guests and let them savor the dark and enchanting flavors of this bewitching elixir.

TIPS

Adjust the sweetness of the brew by adding more or less simple syrup to suit your taste.

Ghostly Elixir

Dive into the spectral realm with our Ghostly Elixir, a chillingly refreshing beverage that's ideal for your Halloween celebration. This eerie concoction combines the tartness of limes, the sweetness of lychees, and a splash of coconut for a hauntingly delicious drink that will send shivers down your spine.

Servings: 4

Preparation time: 10 minutes

Ingredients

1 cup fresh lime juice (about 6-8 limes)

1/2 cup canned lychee juice (from canned lychees)

Lychee fruits (from canned lychees) for garnish

1/2 cup coconut milk

1/4 cup granulated sugar

2 cups sparkling water, chilled

Crushed ice

Lime slices or twists for garnish

Directions

Step 1: In a pitcher, combine the fresh lime juice, canned lychee juice, coconut milk, and granulated sugar. Stir until the sugar is dissolved.

Step 2: Add the chilled sparkling water or club soda to the pitcher and gently mix to combine.

Step 3: Fill glasses with crushed ice.

Step 4: Pour the Ghostly Elixir over the crushed ice in each glass.

Step 5: Garnish each glass with a lychee fruit (you can skewer it on a toothpick for a spooky effect) and a lime slice or twist for a touch of haunting elegance.

Step 6: Serve your Ghostly Elixir to your guests, and let them relish the chillingly delightful flavors of this spectral libation.

TIPS

For an adult version, consider adding a splash of coconut rum or vodka to individual servings.

Swamp Water Smoothie

Embark on a journey into the eerie swamplands with our Swamp Water Smoothie, a hauntingly delicious and nutritious concoction. This chilling green elixir combines the goodness of spinach, the sweetness of tropical fruits, and a touch of mystery to create a smoothie that's both creepy and refreshing.

Servings: 4

Preparation time: 10 minutes

Ingredients

2 cups fresh spinach leaves (packed)

1 cup frozen pineapple chunks

1/2 cup frozen mango chunks

1 banana

1 cup coconut water or coconut milk

1/2 cup Greek yogurt

2 tablespoons honey

Crushed ice

Gummy worms or other creepy candy for garnish

Directions

Step 1: Place the fresh spinach, frozen pineapple chunks, frozen mango chunks, banana, coconut water or coconut milk, Greek yogurt, and honey in a blender.

Step 2: Blend the ingredients until the mixture is smooth and the spinach is fully incorporated.

Step 3: Add crushed ice to the blender and blend again until the smoothie reaches your desired thickness.

Step 4: Pour the eerie green smoothie into glasses.

Step 5: For an extra eerie touch, garnish each glass with gummy worms or other creepy candy.

Step 6: Serve your Swamp Water Smoothie to your guests, and let them sip on the chillingly refreshing flavors of this swamp-inspired concoction.

TIPS

To make your smoothie even spookier, consider using themed straws or cups to add a playful Halloween touch.

TRICK-OR-TREAT GOODIES

Caramel Popcorn Balls

Get ready to roll up a fun and gooey treat with our Caramel Popcorn Balls! These sticky, sweet delights are not only simple to make but also perfect for Halloween parties, family gatherings, or any time you're craving a bit of nostalgia. Customize them with your favorite mix-ins for a unique twist.

Servings: 12 popcorn balls

Prep + Cooking time: 15 minutes + Chilling time

Ingredients

FOR THE CARAMEL SAUCE:

1 cup granulated sugar

1/4 cup unsalted butter

1/4 cup light corn syrup

1/2 cup sweetened condensed milk

1/2 teaspoon vanilla extract

1/4 teaspoon salt

FOR THE POPCORN BALLS:

12 cups popped popcorn (about 1/2 cup unpopped kernels)

Cooking spray

Mix-ins: chopped nuts, mini chocolate chips, dried fruit, candy pieces, etc.

Directions

Step 1: Prepare a large mixing bowl filled with the popped popcorn. Be sure to remove any unpopped kernels.

Step 2: In a medium saucepan, combine the granulated sugar, unsalted butter, light corn syrup, sweetened condensed milk, vanilla extract, and salt.

Step 3: Cook the caramel sauce over medium heat, stirring constantly, until it reaches the soft-ball stage on a candy thermometer (about 235-240°F). This should take about 5 minutes.

Step 4: Once the caramel sauce is ready, immediately pour it over the popped popcorn in the mixing bowl.

Step 5: Quickly and carefully stir the caramel into the popcorn, coating it as evenly as possible. Fold in mix-ins.

Step 6: Coat your hands with cooking spray or butter to prevent sticking, then quickly shape the caramel-coated popcorn into balls. The mixture will be hot, so use caution.

Step 7: Place the caramel popcorn balls on a baking sheet or wax paper to cool and set for about 10-15 minutes.

Step 8: Once the popcorn balls have cooled and set, you can individually wrap them in plastic wrap or wax paper for easy storage or enjoyment.

TIPS

Feel free to get creative with your mix-ins to add extra flavor and texture to your caramel popcorn balls. Mini marshmallows, crushed cookies, or even a touch of sea salt can take these treats to the next level.

Homemade Candy Bars

Unwrap the magic of homemade candy bars with this recipe that lets you create your own sweet confections right in your kitchen. These scrumptious candy bars are customizable, allowing you to experiment with different fillings, coatings, and toppings to craft a unique treat that's perfect for any occasion.

Servings: 12-16

Preparation time: 30 minutes + Chilling time

Ingredients

FOR THE CANDY BASE:

2 cups semisweet chocolate chips

1/2 cup heavy cream

2 tablespoons unsalted butter

1 teaspoon vanilla extract

FOR FILLINGS:

Chopped nuts

Caramel sauce

Marshmallow fluff

Dried fruit

Cookie crumbs

Peanut butter

FOR TOPPINGS:

Additional chocolate chips

Crushed nuts

Shredded coconut

Sprinkles

Directions

Step 1: Prepare a baking dish or tray by lining it with parchment paper, leaving an overhang on the sides for easy removal later.

Step 2: In a microwave-safe bowl or using a double boiler, combine the semisweet chocolate chips, heavy cream, and unsalted butter.

Step 3: Heat the mixture in the microwave, stirring at 30-second intervals. Continue until the mixture is smooth and well combined.

Step 4: Remove the chocolate mixture from the heat and stir in the vanilla extract.

Step 5: Pour half of the chocolate mixture into the prepared baking dish and spread it evenly to create the base layer. Place it in the refrigerator to set for about 30 minutes.

Step 6: Once the base layer has set, add your desired fillings. You can create layers of nuts, caramel sauce, marshmallow fluff, dried fruit, cookie crumbs, or any combination you like.

Step 7: Pour the remaining chocolate mixture over the fillings, covering them completely.

Step 8: Sprinkle with crushed nuts, shredded coconut, and sprinkles over the top layer of chocolate.

Step 9: Place the baking dish back in the refrigerator to chill for an additional 2-3 hours or until the candy bars are fully set.

Step 10: Once the candy bars are set, use the parchment paper overhang to lift them out of the baking dish. Place them on a cutting board.

Step 11: Use a sharp knife to cut the candy bars into your desired size and shape.

Step 12: Store your homemade candy bars in an airtight container in the refrigerator until you're ready to enjoy them.

TIPS

Get creative with your homemade candy bars by experimenting with different combinations of fillings and toppings. You can even drizzle extra melted chocolate on top for an added touch of decadence.

Candy Corn Fudge

Celebrate the sweetness of Halloween with our Candy Corn Fudge, a delightful confection that captures the iconic colors and flavors of the season. This fudge is easy to make and perfect for sharing with friends and family during spooky gatherings or as a festive treat.

Servings: 16 pieces

Preparation time: 15 minutes + Chilling time

Ingredients

2 cups white chocolate chips

1/2 cup sweetened condensed milk

1/4 cup unsalted butter

1/4 teaspoon salt

1/2 teaspoon vanilla extract

1 cup candy corn

Orange and yellow food coloring

Directions

Step 1: Line an 8x8-inch square baking pan with parchment paper, leaving an overhang on two opposite sides for easy lifting later.

Step 2: In a microwave-safe bowl, melt the white chocolate chips, sweetened condensed milk, and unsalted butter together. Heat in 30-second intervals, stirring each time until smooth.

Step 3: Once the mixture is fully melted and smooth, stir in the salt and vanilla extract.

Step 4: Divide the fudge mixture into three equal portions.

Step 5: Leave one portion as is (white). Add orange food coloring to one portion and yellow food coloring to another portion. Stir until the desired colors are achieved, resembling the colors of candy corn.

Step 6: Pour the white fudge mixture into the prepared baking pan and spread it evenly using a spatula.

Step 7: Carefully spread the orange fudge mixture on top of the white layer, followed by the yellow fudge mixture on top of the orange layer.

Step 8: While the fudge is still soft, gently press candy corn into the top layer in rows or patterns.

Step 9: Refrigerate the Candy Corn Fudge for 2-3 hours or until it's completely set.

Step 10: Once set, use the parchment paper overhang to lift the fudge out of the pan.

Step 11: Place the fudge on a cutting board and cut it into squares or rectangles.

Step 12: Serve and enjoy your colorful and festive Candy Corn Fudge!

TIPS

Store any leftover Candy Corn Fudge in an airtight container in the refrigerator to keep it fresh.

Spooky Snack Mix

Create a hauntingly delicious snack that's perfect for Halloween. This mix combines a devilish blend of sweet and salty treats with a touch of eerie charm. It's effortless to make and impossible to resist!

Servings: 12

Preparation time: 10 minutes

Ingredients

FOR THE SPOOKY SNACK MIX:

4 cups popped popcorn (about 1/2 cup unpopped kernels)

2 cups mini pretzels

1 cup candy corn

1 cup Reese's Pieces or other candy-coated chocolates

1 cup chocolate-covered pretzels or other chocolate-covered snacks

1/2 cup roasted salted peanuts or mixed nuts

1/2 cup dried cranberries

FOR THE SPOOKY SEASONING:

1/4 cup unsalted butter, melted

2 tablespoons powdered sugar

1/2 teaspoon cinnamon

1/4 teaspoon nutmeg

1/4 teaspoon ground cloves

Directions

Step 1: Start by preheating your oven to 250°F. Line a large baking sheet with parchment paper or a silicone baking mat.

Step 2: In a large mixing bowl, combine the popped popcorn, mini pretzels, candy corn, Reese's Pieces, chocolate-covered pretzels, and roasted salted peanuts. Add the dried cranberries.

Step 3: In a separate small bowl, prepare the Spooky Seasoning by mixing together the melted unsalted butter, powdered sugar, cinnamon, nutmeg, and ground cloves.

Step 4: Drizzle the Spooky Seasoning in the large mixing bowl over the snack mix.

Step 5: Gently toss and stir the snack mix to evenly coat it with the Spooky Seasoning.

Step 6: Spread the coated snack mix onto the prepared baking sheet in an even layer.

Step 7: Bake in the oven for about 45 minutes, stirring every 15 minutes to ensure even coating and prevent burning.

Step 8: Remove the Spooky Snack Mix from the oven and let it cool completely on the baking sheet.

Step 9: Once cooled, break the snack mix into chunks and serve in individual bowls or a large communal bowl.

TIPS

Customize your Spooky Snack Mix by adding your favorite Halloween-themed candies, nuts, or dried fruits. You can also adjust the Spooky Seasoning to your taste by adding more or less of the spices.

POST-HALLOWEEN BREAKFAST

Candy Overload Pancakes

Indulge your sweet tooth with a decadent breakfast treat that's perfect for special occasions or satisfying your cravings on Halloween morning. These fluffy pancakes are loaded with your favorite candies, making them an irresistible and delightful way to start the day.

Servings: 4

Prep + Cooking time: 30 minutes

Ingredients

FOR THE CANDY OVERLOAD PANCAKES:

1 1/2 cups all-purpose flour

2 tablespoons granulated sugar

2 teaspoons baking powder

1/2 teaspoon baking soda

1/4 teaspoon salt

1 1/4 cups buttermilk

1/4 cup unsalted butter, melted

2 large eggs

1 teaspoon vanilla extract

1 cup mixed Halloween candies

FOR TOPPINGS:

Whipped cream

Maple syrup

Additional candy pieces for garnish

Sprinkles

Directions

Step 1: In a large mixing bowl, whisk together the all-purpose flour, granulated sugar, baking powder, baking soda, and salt.

Step 2: In a separate bowl, whisk together the buttermilk, melted unsalted butter, eggs, and vanilla extract.

Step 3: Pour the wet ingredients into the dry ingredients and stir until just combined. Be careful not to overmix; a few lumps in the batter are okay.

Step 4: Gently fold in the mixed Halloween candies of your choice. Save a small portion to sprinkle on top of the pancakes.

Step 5: Preheat a griddle or non-stick skillet over medium heat and lightly grease it with cooking spray or a small amount of butter.

Step 6: Pour 1/4 cup portions of pancake batter onto the griddle, leaving some space between each pancake.

Step 7: Cook until the pancakes start to bubble on top and the edges look set, about 2-3 minutes.

Step 8: Carefully flip the pancakes and cook for an additional 1-2 minutes or until they are golden brown and cooked through.

Step 9: Remove the pancakes from the griddle and keep them warm.

Step 10: Top your Candy Overload Pancakes with whipped cream, additional candy pieces, maple syrup, and sprinkles.

TIPS

Be creative with your candy choices to match your favorite Halloween flavors. You can also add crushed cookies or graham cracker crumbs for extra texture.

Witches' Brew Coffee

Fuel your mystical adventures with a cup of Witches' Brew Coffee, a bewitching brew that's perfect for Halloween mornings, or anytime you want a touch of enchantment in your cup. This dark, aromatic coffee is infused with intriguing flavors and topped with a wickedly delightful cream.

Servings: 4

Preparation time: 10 minutes

Ingredients

FOR THE WITCHES' BREW COFFEE:

4 cups freshly brewed dark roast coffee

1/4 cup unsweetened cocoa powder

1/4 cup granulated sugar

1/2 teaspoon ground cinnamon

1/4 teaspoon ground nutmeg

1/4 teaspoon ground cloves

1/4 teaspoon vanilla extract

FOR THE WICKED CREAM TOPPING:

1 cup heavy cream

2 tablespoons powdered sugar

1/2 teaspoon black food coloring

FOR GARNISH:

Chocolate shavings or cocoa powder

Witch hat-shaped chocolate cookies or cinnamon sticks

Directions

Step 1: In a small bowl, combine the unsweetened cocoa powder, granulated sugar, ground cinnamon, ground nutmeg, and ground cloves.

Step 2: Brew 4 cups of dark roast coffee using your preferred method.

Step 3: While the coffee is still hot, add the cocoa mixture to it and stir until fully dissolved. Stir in the vanilla extract as well.

Step 4: In a separate bowl, whip the heavy cream and powdered sugar together until it forms stiff peaks.

Step 5: Add the black food coloring to the whipped cream and gently fold it in until the cream turns a wicked shade of black.

Step 6: Pour the Witches' Brew Coffee into individual cups or mugs.

Step 7: Carefully spoon a dollop of the wicked black cream on top of each cup of coffee.

Step 8: Garnish with chocolate shavings, a sprinkle of cocoa powder, or witch hat-shaped chocolate cookies as a playful touch.

Step 9: Serve your Witches' Brew Coffee while it's hot and enchanting.

TIPS

Adjust the sweetness of your Witches' Brew Coffee by adding more or less sugar to the cocoa mixture. You can also customize the flavor by experimenting with different spices or flavored coffee syrups.

Ghostly Crepe Art

Add a playful and spooky twist to your breakfast routine with Ghostly Pancake Art. These ghost-shaped pancakes are not only a fun and creative way to start your day but also a delightful treat for Halloween or any ghostly-themed occasion. Get ready to turn your breakfast into a ghost hunt!

Servings: 12

Prep + Cooking time: 30 minutes

Ingredients

Your favorite pancake batter

Cooking spray or melted butter

Whipped cream

Blueberries (for eyes)

Directions

Step 1: Prepare your favorite pancake batter according to the recipe or package instructions.

Step 2: Heat a non-stick griddle or skillet over medium-low heat and lightly grease it with cooking spray or melted butter.

Step 3: Pour a small amount of pancake batter onto the griddle to create the head of the ghost.

Step 4: Use a spoon or squeeze bottle to add a tail-like extension to the bottom of the pancake, forming the ghost's body.

Step 5: Cook the pancake until bubbles form on the surface and the edges start to look set.

Step 6: Carefully flip the pancake using a spatula and cook the other side until it's golden brown.

Step 7: Remove the ghost-shaped pancake from the griddle and place it on a serving plate.

Step 8: To create the ghost's eyes, add two mini chocolate chips or blueberries as eyes on the head of the pancake.

Step 9: Use whipped cream to make a spooky swirl or cloud-like shape around the ghost, creating the appearance of a ghostly aura.

Step 10: Serve your Ghostly Pancake Art with a smile, and let the ghost hunt begin!

TIPS

Get creative with your Ghostly Pancake Art by adding other toppings like fresh berries, sliced bananas, or a drizzle of chocolate syrup for added flavor and character.

Pumpkin Spice French Toast

Wake up to the warm and comforting flavors of fall with our Pumpkin Spice French Toast. This delightful breakfast dish combines the seasonal goodness of pumpkin, spices, and creamy custard, transforming ordinary French toast into a heavenly autumn treat.

Servings: 4

Prep + Cooking time: 30 minutes

Ingredients

FOR THE PUMPKIN SPICE FRENCH TOAST:

8 slices of thick bread

4 large eggs

1/2 cup pumpkin puree

1/2 cup whole milk

1/4 cup granulated sugar

1 teaspoon vanilla extract

1 teaspoon ground cinnamon

1/2 teaspoon ground nutmeg

1/4 teaspoon ground cloves

1/4 teaspoon ground ginger

A pinch of salt

Unsalted butter for cooking

FOR SERVING:

Maple syrup

Whipped cream

Chopped pecans or walnuts

Powdered sugar

Directions

Step 1: In a large mixing bowl, whisk together the eggs, pumpkin puree, whole milk, granulated sugar, vanilla extract, ground cinnamon, ground nutmeg, ground cloves, ground ginger, and a pinch of salt. Mix until the ingredients are well combined.

Step 2: Heat a non-stick skillet or griddle over medium heat and add a small amount of unsalted butter to coat the surface.

Step 3: Dip each slice of bread into the pumpkin spice custard mixture, making sure both sides are evenly coated.

Step 4: Place the coated bread slices on the preheated skillet or griddle and cook until golden brown on both sides, about 2-3 minutes per side. Add more butter to the skillet as needed.

Step 5: Remove the Pumpkin Spice French Toast from the skillet and keep it warm.

Step 6: Serve the French toast slices with a drizzle of maple syrup. Top with whipped cream, chopped pecans or walnuts, and a dusting of powdered sugar.

TIPS

For an extra dose of autumn flavor, you can add a sprinkle of cinnamon or a dollop of pumpkin puree on top of each serving.

CONCLUSION

I hope that "Boo-Tastic Halloween Cookbook" has served as your trusty companion throughout this spine-tingling culinary adventure. Our aim has been to enchant your senses, elevate your Halloween gatherings, and spark your creativity in the kitchen.

Now, as you prepare to wrap up your spooktacular night, I invite you to reflect on the magic of Halloween cuisine. From bewitching appetizers to monstrous main courses and sinisterly sweet desserts, each recipe was crafted to evoke the essence of this haunting holiday.

But your journey doesn't end here. I encourage you to continue experimenting with these recipes, sharing them with family and friends, and creating new Halloween traditions. Your kitchen is a cauldron of endless possibilities, and every year offers a chance to brew up fresh and captivating delights.

So, as you embark on your my Halloween adventures, don't forget to "share your Halloween creations" with the world. Whether it's through a haunted feast with loved ones, a spooky costume party, or simply sharing your culinary masterpieces on social media, your creativity can inspire others to embrace the enchantment of Halloween.

I wish you many more years of magical and delicious Halloween celebrations filled with laughter, frights, and unforgettable flavors.

Thank you for joining us on this culinary journey, and may your Halloween nights always be spooktacular!

Create Your Halloween Recipes

Recipe Name:

Ingredients

Directions

Recipe Name:

Ingredients

Directions

Recipe Name:

Ingredients

Directions

Recipe Name:

Ingredients

Directions

Recipe Name:

Ingredients

Directions

Recipe Name:

Ingredients

_____

_____

_____

_____

_____

Directions

_____

_____

_____

_____

_____

_____

_____

_____

_____

Recipe Name:

Ingredients

Directions

Recipe Name:

Ingredients

_____

_____

_____

_____

_____

Directions

_____

_____

_____

_____

_____

_____

_____

_____

Recipe Name:

Ingredients

Directions

Recipe Name:

Ingredients

Directions

Recipe Name:

Ingredients

Directions

Recipe Name:

Ingredients

Directions

Recipe Name:

Ingredients

Directions

Recipe Name:

Ingredients

_____

_____

_____

_____

_____

Directions

_____

_____

_____

_____

_____

_____

_____

_____

_____

Recipe Name:

Ingredients

_____

_____

_____

_____

Directions

_____

_____

_____

_____

_____

_____

_____

Recipe Name:

Ingredients

Directions